A wonderful plant, full of natural medicinal properties

Dr. Rajeev Sharma

MANOJ PUBLICATIONS

© *All Rights Reserved*

Publishers :

Manoj Publications
761, Main Road, Burari, Delhi-110084
Ph.: 27611116, 27611349, Fax : 27611546
Mobile : 9868112194
E-mail : *info@manojpublications.com*
Website : *www.manojpublications.com*

Showroom :

Manoj Publications
1583-84, Dariba Kalan, Chandni Chowk,
Delhi-110006
Ph. : 23262174, 23268216, Mobile : 9818753569

ISBN : 978-81-310-0827-0

Fourth Edition : 2012

₹ 50

Printers :
Jai Maya Offset
Jhilmil Industrial Area, Delhi-110095

Aloe Vera : Dr. Rajeev Sharma

PREFACE

Thanks to nature for the Aloe Vera plant for its characteristic goodness that it bestows on humanity in the fields of medicine and beauty. The role of Aloe Vera does not limit itself to only cosmetology and skin care but surprisingly a remedy to many ailments. The health benefits of aloe Vera are on the rise with its miraculous healing qualities.

The aloe drink is used as a tonic for curing arthritis, diabetes and high cholesterol. Aloe properties aid in steadying blood sugar levels. It also works its way in building good immunity.

Aloe is also used to cure skin ailments and wounds. Aloe gels are used to treat cuts, bruises, wounds and scrapes. Aloe contains magnesium lactate, an itch inhibitor bringing in relief to insect bites, acne, sunburns and rashes. Aloe effectively treats warts and also lesions inside and outside the mouth. Its healing quality can even cure psoriasis.

Aloe is widely accepted and appreciated in the cosmetic word. It is used as an anti-wrinkle treatment due to its effectiveness in stimulating the production of collagen and elastin that helps in keeping aging at bay. As a cleanser it helps in removing dead cells. It is an effective moisturiser for the skin. Its properties lighten skin pigmentation thereby reducing the intensity of dark spots and left over pimple marks.

In this book the subject is covered to its full. We try our best to cover every aspect of Aloe Vera, its medicinal and industrial use along with home remedies.

—*Publishers*

CONTENTS

INTRODUCTION

Besure Aloe Vera, *Ghritkumari, Gheekunwar,* the names are many but they all belong to one miracle plant *Aloe barbadensis.* It's a wonder plant with health benefits so myriad and astounding that hardly any part of human body remains that is not influenced by its healing touch. From being a natural fighter against all sorts of infection, an efficient anti-oxidant to help in all digestion related problems, arthritis, stress, diabetes, cancer, an enhancer of beauty, Aloe has been proved by research to be a plant of amazing medicinal properties.

The medicinal value of the plant recognized for centuries for its remarkable properties, lies in the gel like pulp obtained on peeling the leaves. Its juice has cooling properties, is anabolic in action, a fighter of *pitta* (bile) and guards against fever, skin diseases, burns, ulcers, boils eruptions etc. Aloe's active principle 'aloin' is responsible for its unique digestive properties. Though it would be too exhaustive to enumerate its health benefits, the areas in which Aloe plant extract helps is summarized, in short, as under Antiseptic, Anti-bactericidal. Aloe Vera produces six antiseptic agents with anti-microbial properties and if its juice is taken on daily basis is protective against diseases.

Thanks to nature for the Aloe Vera plant for its characteristic goodness that it bestows on humanity in the fields of medicine and beauty. The role of Aloe Vera does not limit itself to only cosmetology and skin care but surprisingly a remedy to many ailments. The health benefits of Aloe Vera are on the rise with its miraculous healing qualities.

The Aloe plant belongs to the onion/garlic family and there are about three hundred species of Aloe Vera. However the most important one is Aloe barbadensis Miller. Aloe contains almost 20 amino acids, vital minerals like calcium, magnesium and sodium in sufficient quantities, enzymes, vitamins, polysaccharides, nitrogen and other components which make it a miracle substance. Aloe Vera is found to have medicinal and cosmetic properties. Aloe Vera properties find expressions in Aloe wound creams, moisturizers, cleansers, gels, and health drinks etc.

The Aloe drink is used as a tonic for curing arthritis, diabetes and high cholesterol. Aloe properties aid in maintaining blood sugar levels. It also works its way in building good immunity. Aloe gels and sprays help in reducing muscle and joint pains as well as regressing the pain caused by arthritis. It helps in decreasing the cholesterol, blood fat lipid levels and triglycerides that are some of the major causes for heart problems.

Aloe's curative properties help a great deal in curing digestive disorders. It effectively cures ulcers, heartburns, irritable bowl syndrome and indigestion. It is also used as a laxative and is said to have anti-inflammatory properties that help in reducing the amount of the stomach juices secreted. Its properties are capable of destroying the bacteria or parasites in the intestines.

Aloe is also used to cure skin ailments and wounds. Aloe gels are used to treat cuts, bruises, wounds and scrapes. Aloe contains magnesium lactate, an itch inhibitor bringing in relief to insect bites, acne, sunburns and rashes. Aloe effectively treats warts and also lesions inside and outside the mouth. Its healing quality can even cure psoriasis.

Aloe is widely accepted and appreciated in the cosmetic word. It is used as an anti-wrinkle treatment due to its

effectiveness in stimulating the production of collagen and elastin that helps in keeping aging at bay. As a cleanser it helps in removing dead cells. It is an effective moisturiser for the skin. Its properties lighten skin pigmentation thereby reducing the intensity of dark spots and left over pimple marks.

□□

HISTORY OF ALOE VERA

Between 1840 and 1850 the Aloe Vera plant has been brought to Aruba and is since then cultivated in Aruba on a large scale. Aruba had the ideal climate for the Aloe plant and very soon thousands of acres of Aloe were grown and many Aruban families lived from the harvest of the Aloe Vera, in those days only for the export of the raw material for laxatives.

In the literature on Aloe the quality of the Aruba Aloes were undisputedly superior to other Aloes and this was also the reason that at the beginning of our century Aruba became the largest exporter of Aloe vera products in the world and soon earned the name 'Island of Aloe'.

In the code of arms of Aruba an Aloe plant is shown and the official name for the laxative raw material is 'Curacao Aloes', named after the harbour from where the Aruba Aloes were shipped all over the world (Curacao itself had virtually no Aloe production).

At the end of the fifties, new, synthetic laxatives replaced the Aloes worldwide and other industries (oil refining and tourism) replaced the Aloe industry in Aruba. The Aloe fields, however, remained, and still Aruba was the 'Island of Aloe' and the Aloe plant stayed in the code of arms of Aruba. Aruba had set the record to be able to be the largest supplier in the world of the best Aloe.

When the parenchyma (the mucilaginous material in the leaves) of the leaves is removed, this so called 'gel-filet' is grinned and the fibers are removed. An opalescent liquid remains that is commonly called 'Aloe Vera Gel' and after preservation this is the liquid that is used in skin preparations and health drinks.

Aloe Vera Gel consists for 99.3% of water. The remaining 0.7% are the solids that consist for a large part of polysaccharides of the glucose and mannose type. Together with the enzymes and amino acids in the gel they give the gel the special properties as a skin care product.

The gel stimulates cell growth and as such enhances the restoration of damaged skin. It moisturizes the skin because it has a water holding capacity. This moist on the skin also has a cooling effect. As a drink it protects the mucous membrane of the stomach especially when irritated or damaged.

□□

ALOEA VERA

Aloe Vera has been a craze among consumer products in recent times. Soaps, shampoos, creams, lotions and almost everything of daily use come with Aloe Vera. Intestinal ailments, skin disorders and almost all ailments including cancer and even AIDS are claimed to be curable by extracts of this wonder plant. Diascorides, the ancient physician who accompanied the Roman army was an ardent fan of this plant and he had prima facie knowledge of its enormous power to heal wounds of soldiers injured in war. The prominent Greek Scientist Celsius was also a supporter of this wonder plant. Kopra's *The Indigenous Drugs of India* a 400 year old book also have references Aloe Vera. Let us see what this magical plant is and how much useful it actually is?

Some facts about the Plant

Though Aloe Vera is a native of the Tropical Africa it grows even in cold areas and is widely cultivated for its medicinal extracts all through the world; it belongs to the plant family Liliaceae (known after the family's popular member Lily) and scientists call it Aloe vera barbandensis. Aloe Vera is a succulent plant with rosette of thick tapering leaves with serrate margins and bell or tubular shaped flowers. There are about 240 varieties of this species found in various parts of the world. Its succulent leaves are composed of 95% water and juice extracted from it has strong laxative properties had been in use in several African and Asian countries for years. Aloe Vera is a commercially cultivated in Texas, Florida and California, in Oklahoma they are massively grown in special green houses.

Aloe gel and Aloe juice

The succulent leaves yield two types of extracts—Aloe gel and latex, the jelly like light juice that exudes from soft parenchyma cell of leaves is the Aloe jelly and that got from the peri-cycle tubules just below leaves is called Aloe latex (or Aloe juice). Both these extracts are similar in quality and contain various minerals, vitamins, amino acids, calcium, potassium and zinc etc all essential materials for the well being of human body. Physicians have approved the extracts having curative properties to heal skin disorders, cuts, burns, eczema etc. Aloe gel can eliminate warts and such external growths on skin. Aloe gel mixed with vitamin E and collagen makes excellent skin-cream that can retain elasticity of the skin even at old age.

Believe it or not!

Mixing Aloe gel with warm water makes a good gargle medium that is good to keep of foul mouth odour; it can cure mouth ulcers as well. This if taken in can cure constipation and heals intestinal wounds, infections, irritable bowel syndrome and related diseases. Colitis, peptic ulcer, troubles related to the small and large intestine are also found to disappear by the use of this mixture. Aloe Vera is richly endowed with natural alkaline compounds and they protect stomach and intestinal skin from excessive acidity of the intestinal juices and its corrosive effects on the skin.

Even as a Food

Aloe Vera is used a food by people in the Thar Desert of Rajasthan, they cook it with seeds of fenugreek (fenugreek is also having some medicinal properties).

The plant of Immortality

Aloe Vera prefers salty water (can grow even if irrigated with sea-water), it flourishes at gardens with occasional irrigation with salted water. Aloe Vera had prominent roles in the folklores of Japan, Philippines but it was the Spanish which spread this plant to South America and the Caribbean. In ancient Egypt Aloe Vera plant was so popular that they called it 'the immortal plant' and pictured in on the walls of their tombs. They believed that use of this plant can retain external youth!

Was in Cleopatra's shopping list

It may be in every girl's dream to be as beautiful as Cleopatra the serpent beauty of the yore, no problem there is a way use the beauty-potion Cleopatra used; it was nothing else but Aloe Vera extract that enhanced and sustained the enchanting beauty of Queen Cleopatra. Alexander The Great used this for healing wounds of soldiers. Chinese applied it on the skin-ailments, warts, psoriasis, and allergies, where as tribals of Africa applied Aloe Vera juice on their body to escape excessive perspiration and loss of water.

Some good news

Some of the findings are good news to those with heart and related ailments, experiments have proved that Aloe gel can reduce the possibility of heart attacks by strengthening walls of heart and blood vessels. Consumption of Isabgol and Aloe gel along with food has been found to reduce Lipids, serum cholesterol, triglycerides and fasting blood sugar as well as blood sugar after food. There are even reports that when Aloe Vera gel was administered in animals with diabetes their blood sugar level was found lowered.

□□

NATURE AND CONSTITUENTS
OF ALOE VERA

Aloe Vera is a succulent that belongs to the liliaceae family. It is one of the 250 known species of aloes, referred to by the scientific terms of Aloe Vera and Aloe barbadensis. Called *Ghritakumari* in Sanskrit, it is commonly known as Aloe, Aloe Vera, Barbados Aloe, Sabila and Pita Sabila. Akin to cactus in appearance, it grows naturally in Africa, America, Europe and Asia. The ideal environment for cultivating Aloe Vera is a tropical climate and low rainfall.

The mature plant will grow up to a height of twenty-five feet. It has fibrous roots and bright green gelatinous leaves, enveloped in a fine layer of a yellow liquid or sap. Aloe Vera produces flowers and seeds from the same root structure year after year. The yellow to purplish drooping flowers grow in a long raceme at the top of the flower stalk. The fruit is a triangular capsule containing numerous seeds.

The Constituents

The various constituent elements found in Aloe Vera include:

Vitamins : Beta-carotene, Vitamin-B1, Vitamin-B2, Folic acid, Vitamin-C, Vitamin-B3, Vitamin-B6,Vitamin-E and Choline.

Minerals : Calcium, Magnesium, Sodium, Copper, Iron, Manganese, Potassium, Zinc, Chromium and Chlorine.

Amino Acids : Lysine, Threonine, Valine, Methionine, Leucine, Isoleucine, Phenylaianine, Tryptophane, Histidine,

Arginine, Hydroxy Proline, Aspartic acid, Serine, Glutamic acid, Proline, Glycerine, Alanine, Cystine and Tyrosine.

Anthraquinones : Aloin, Isobarbaloin, Barbaloin, Cinnamic acid, Emodin, Aloe Emodin, Ester of Cinnamic acid, Anthracene, Antranol, Aloetic acid, Ethereal oils, Resistannols and Crysophanic acid.

Mono and polysaccharides : Cellulose, Glucose, Mannose, Galactose, Aldonentose, L-rhamnose, Uronic acid, Xylose, Glucuronic acid and Arabinose.

Enzymes : Oxidase, Amylase, Catalase, Lipase and Alinase.

Applications / Uses : The important therapeutic uses of Aloe Vera include :

❐ The long chain mannan polysaccharides in it helps activate and boost the Immune System.

❐ The magnesium lactate and salicylates in it effectively avert Allergies, Sinusitis and Bronchitis.

❐ The molecules in it act as anti-inflammatory agent, a cure for arthritis, and promote good circulation for the heart and nervous system.

❐ The polysaccharides in it bring down the bodies serum lipids, and thus lower triglyceride and LDL level (bad cholesterol) and increase of HDL (good cholesterol).

❐ As an antioxidant, it guards against damage by free radicals and unwarranted toxins in the body. It also regulates blood pressure, and acts in rheumatism, arthritis, and infections of the kidney, the urinary tract and the prostate.

❐ By the combined and synergic effect of the various ingredients in it, it aids in treatment of peptic ulcers, stomach disorders, acidity, indigestion, gastritis and ulcers, colitis and haemorrhoids, cirrhosis, hepatitis and diabetes.

❐❐

CULTIVATION & DEMAND

A conservative estimate puts the monetary value of current Global trade in medicinal plants at over US $ 60 billion. With the increasing interest in 'natural' products across the world and the resultant upsurge in the demand for medicinal plants, this trade is expected to grow up to US $ 5 trillion by the year 2050. Aloe Vera is among the few medicinal plants by virtue of their extensive medicinal, nutraceutical and other uses enjoy a major chunk of the market across the globe. The major markets for Aloe Vera and its extracts are Australia, US and the entire Europe. Despite the ideal climatic conditions for the cultivation of Aloe Vera, we have not been able to exploit the excellent potential of the miraculous medicinal plant. The reasons are simple—lack of cultivation and processing know-how.

Given the exponentially growing demand for it in the international market, Aloe Vera presents the finest commercial opportunity among the various medicinal plants. Also, India is among the few countries gifted with the unique geographical features essential for cultivation of Aloe Vera and other high potential medicinal plants. Yet, the country has not realized and reaped the full potential of such plants. The reason is simple—lack of the requisite expertise. Fortunately, the technology is now accessible to individual and corporate entrepreneurs to make the most of Aloe Vera through mainstream cultivation.

Cultivation Process

Though Aloe Vera can be cultivated on any soil for 'dry land management', sandy loamy soil is the best suited for it. Aloe Vera is generally propagated by root suckers by carefully digging out without damaging the parent plant and planting it in the main field. It can also be propagated through rhizome cuttings, By digging out the rhizomes after the harvest of the crop and making them into 5-6 cm length cuttings with a minimum of 2-3 nodes on them. Then they are rooted in specially prepared sand beds or containers. The plant is ready for transplanting after the appearance of the first sprouts. The process of cultivating Aloe Vera involves the following process:

❑ The ground is to be carefully prepared to keep free from weeds and the soil is ideally kept ideally slightly acidic. The soil should be supplied supplement in the form of ammonium nitrate every year.

❑ The plants are set spaced out by 31 inches in rows and between the rows. At that rate, about 5,000 plants are set per acre. An 8-12 inch Aloe pop would take about 18-24 months to fully mature.

❑ The plants, in a year's time, would bear flowers that are bright yellow in colour. The leaves are 1 to 2 feet long and are cut without causing damage to the plant, so that it lasts for several years.

16

- The crop can be harvested 4 times a year. At the rate of 3 leaves cut from each plant, about 12 leaves are the harvest per plant per year. On an average, the yield per acre annually is about 60,000 kg.

- The leaves cut off close to the plant are placed immediately, with the cut end downwards, in a V-shaped wooden trough of about 4 feet long and 12 to 18 inches deep.

- The wooden trough is set on a sharp incline so that the juice, which trickles from the leaves very rapidly, flows down its sides, and finally escapes by a hole at its lower end into a vessel placed beneath.

- It takes about a quarter of an hour to cut leaves enough to fill a trough. The troughs are so distributed as to be easily accessible to the cutters.

- The leaves are neither infused nor boiled, nor is any use afterwards made of them except for manure. When the vessels receiving the juice become filled, the latter is removed to a cask or reserved for evaporation. This may be done at once, or it may be delayed for weeks or even months.

- The evaporation is generally conducted in a copper vessel; at the bottom of this is a large ladle, into which the impurities sink, and are from time to time removed as the boiling goes on.

- As soon as the inspissation has reached the proper point, which is determined solely by the experienced eye of the workman, the thickened juice is poured into large gourds or into boxes, and allowed to harden.

□□

USES OF ALOE VERA

Aloe Vera belongs to lily family and looks like a cactus. More than two hundreds Aloe Vera species can be found and many of them are effective and treated like nutritious. Aloe Vera Barbadensis is beneficial specie.

It has been utilized for health; medical properties, beauty and skin care for many centuries. Aloe Vera plant is regarded as universal panacea, the wand of heaven and the plant of immortality by several scientists and researchers.

Aloe Vera leaves are smooth and rubbery in touching from interior and exterior.

There are large numbers of uses of Aloe Vera and mostly they are utilized as a medication and food preservative. The various Aloe Vera uses included the following :

❒ Aloe Vera is beneficial in the reducing of scalp care, stings, sunburns, sore muscles, scrapes, scalds, psoriasis, acne, burns, arthritis, sprains, bruises, cold-sores and abrasions.

❒ It is useful to treat various skin diseases.

❒ Aloe Vera is utilized in lotions, capsule, gel, creams, spray, liquid etc.

❒ It assists in healing blisters and offers relaxation from itching.

❒ Aloe Vera juices are taken to treat any digestive diseases, ulcers and heartburn.

❒ It decreases the intensity of pigmentation and removes the dark spots from the face.

- Aloe Vera juice decreases the quantity of stomach juices and acts like an anti-inflammatory.
- It is very beneficial in the penetration of healthy matters.
- Muscle pain and joints pain is caused because of arthritis and decreased by using Aloe Vera gels or sprays.
- It is useful to remove dead cells and applied like a moisturizer.
- It is useful to stimulate the creation of collagen and elastin that are essential to prevent the aging of the skin.
- Aloe Vera extract is beneficial to reduce the levels of blood sugar.
- It is beneficial in curing such as anti-fungal, anti-bacterial and anti-oxidant properties.
- Aloe Vera gel offers benefit to decrease the levels of blood fat lipid, triglycerides and cholesterol.
- Many patients take Aloe Vera drink like a tonic.
- It breaks down the fat globules and is useful to decrease obesity.

HEALTH BENEFITS OF ALOE VERA

Thanks to nature for the Aloe Vera plant for its characteristic goodness that it bestows on humanity in the fields of medicine and beauty. The role of Aloe Vera does not limit itself to only cosmetology and skin care but surprisingly a remedy to many ailments. The health benefits of Aloe Vera on the rise with its miraculous healing qualities.

The Aloe plant belongs to the onion/garlic family and there are about three hundred species of Aloe Vera. However the most important one is Aloebadensis Miller. Aloe contain almost 20 amino acids, vital minerals like calcium, magnesium and sodium in sufficient quantities, enzymes, vitamins, polysaccharides, nitrogen and other components which make it a miracle substance. Aloe Vera is found to have medicinal and cosmetic properties. Aloe Vera properties find expressions in Aloe wound creams, moisturizers, cleansers, gels, health drinks etc.

The Aloe drink is used as a tonic for curing arthritis, diabetes and high cholesterol. Aloe properties aid in steadying blood sugar levels. It also works its way in building good immunity. Aloe gels and sprays help in reducing muscle and joint pains as well as regressing the pain caused by arthritis. It helps in decreasing the cholesterol, blood fat lipid levels and triglycerides that are some of the major causes for heart problems.

Aleo's curative properties help a great deal in curing digestive disorders. It effectively cures ulcers, heartburns, irritable bowl syndrome and indigestion. It is also used as a laxative and is said to have anti-inflammatory properties

20

that help in reducing the amount of the stomach juices secreted. Its properties are capable of destroying the bacteria of parasites in the intestines.

Aloe is also used to cure skin ailments and wounds. Aloe gels are used to treat cuts, bruises, wounds and scrapes. Aloe contains magnesium lactate, an itch inhibitor bringing in relief to insect bites, acne, sunburns and rashes. Aloe effectively treats warts and also lesions inside and outside the mouth. Its healing quality can even cure psoriasis.

Aloe is widely accepted and appreciated in the cosmetic word. It is used as an anti-wrinkle treatment due to its effectiveness in stimulating the production of collagen and elastin that helps in keeping aging at bay. As a cleanser it helps in removing dead cells. It is an effective moisturizer for the skin. Its properties lighten skin pigmentation thereby reducing the intensity of dark spots and left over pimple marks.

The health benefits of Aloe Vera can help everyone—adults, children, and yes even pets. Remember, Aloe Vera is a very popular deionifier.

The major health benefit of Aloe Vera is its natural balance. There is no single ingredient that makes Aloe Vera potent and healthful.

Thankfully, the ingredients in Aloe Vera are more effective together as nature intended, than any single element taken by itself.

Aloe Vera's effects cannot be synthesized easily in a laboratory which is great for us because the day that happens Aloe Vera will likely become too expensive for most of us to buy and use on a daily basis.

Aloe Vera's 'Natural Balance' is the key it makes the plant useful across a wide spectrum of circumstances. And because the various elements that make Aloe effective are nutrients rather than drugs, Aloe juice can complement medical treatments.

In fact some cancer patients state that Aloe Vera seems to reduce nausea, increase energy, and may help to minimize low blood counts caused by chemotherapy or radiation.

The possible health benefit of Aloe Vera gel and juice include :

❐ Speeds healing tensile strength and repair of damaged skin wounds, burns and other injuries.

❐ Hold moisture and adds flexibility to retard aging.

❐ Fights infections with its antibacterial properties including fungus, bacteria.

❐ Tightens and balances skin through astringent properties.

❐ Moisturizes by carrying added emollients into the skin up to seven layers.

❐ With natural anti-inflammatory agents reduces pain.

❐ Minimizes scarring and may reverse scars less than five years old.

❐ Sooth skin injured by burns, irritations, cuts and insect bites.

❐ When taken internally assists with constipation, diarrhoea and other intestinal problems.

❐ Speed and improve general healing when taken internally.

❐ Increases the availability of oxygen to the skin.

❐ Relieve itching and swelling of irritated skin.

❐ Improve the effectiveness of sun screen products.

Aloe Vera is non toxic it is not a drug it is not a medicine and is not intended to replace any drugs or medicine but documents and experiences show that when people use a product or drink the juice for whatever reason; Aloe Vera works.

There are no lack of testimonials to Aloe Vera's marvellous benefits and the varied health benefits of Aloe Vera make it valuable enough for everyone to keep on hand. To gain the most therapeutic support wise to use a quality Aloe Vera product.

The established benefits of Aloe Vera are :

Protector of Human Immune System : The whole leaf extract galvanizes the cells of immune system. The phagocytes increase their scavenging activities, thus cleansing the body and kicking off a whole cascade of protective actions which strengthen immunity.

Improves Digestive System : Research work carried out over the years points conclusively that Aloe juice helps in digestive disorders. Constipation, diarrhoea, indigestion, irritable bowel syndrome etc are cured by the flushing action. The deposits of toxins and unwanted substances in our diet which keep accumulating in intestines prevent the absorption of essential nutrients causing nutritional deficiency, lethargy, constipation, lower backache. Aloe juice helps flush out these residues boosting the digestion and giving a greater feeling of well-being.

Arthritis : Being a stimulant to the immune system, a powerful anti-inflammatory, an analgesic and able to speed up cell growth, it repairs arthritis damaged tissue. While conventional allopathic treatment only relieves pain, Aloe Vera juice taken internally and applied externally helps in repair process by regenerating cells and detoxifying the affected area. Aloe Vera fights stress. The stress filled life of today cause bio-chemical and physiological changes in the body, making us susceptible to diseases and dysfunction. Aloe Vera juice is just the thing to get our machinery smoothly and effectively going.

Cancer : Aloe juice enables the body to heal itself from cancer and the damage done by radio and chemotherapy which destroy healthy immune cells crucial to the recovery.

Diabetes : It lowers glucose and tri-glyceride levels in diabetic patients. Effects can be seen from the second week of the treatment.

Hepatitis : Extract of Aloe juice has been shown to have beneficial effects on liver and alleviate symptoms considerably in chronic hepatitis patients.

Heart Disease : Addition of Isabgol and Aloe Vera juice to the diet of patients of angina pectoris, results in marked reduction of serum cholesterol and tri-glycerides and increase in level of HDL.

AIDS : A daily dose of min. 1200 mg. of active ingredients of Aloe Vera showed substantial improvement in AIDS symptoms. Says Dr. Pulse, "Aloe is to an AIDS patient as insulin is to a diabetic."

Wound and Skin Disease : Aloe Vera gel is excellent for easing first degree burns, relieves inflammation and accelerates healing. Aloe Vera gel has anti-fungal, anti-bacterial and anti-viral effects and helps heal minor wounds. It lessens painful effects of shingles, reduces symptoms of psoriasis and eases heartburns and ulcers.

Aloe Vera for Kids : Aloe Vera can be an important ingredient of medicine chest. Children can take Aloe Vera juice as it helps heal on the outside and inside. It soothes stomach upset. It takes the pain out of burns and bites and the growth factors in its yellow sap stimulate new cell growth almost miraculously. Aloe helps by decreasing allergies and colds, lessens laboured breathing, gives calmer energy, better digestion and heal thier skin. Infact, kids and Aloe Vera go together wonderfully.

Beauty Care : Once a beauty arsenal of Cleopatra, today Aloe Vera is showing up as a main ingredient in cosmetic industry. It is one herb which can be used almost as freely as water on skin. Mixed with selected essential oils, it makes for excellent skin smoother and moisturizer, sun block lotion plus a whole range of beauty products.

No wonder then that Aloe Vera is referred to as the 'Miracle Plant'. From being an antiseptic, anti-inflammatory and a cure for heartburns to helping relieve the symptoms of severe illnesses like cancer and diabetes, to being a beauty aid and health nourisher, this ancient Indian herb has it all. Known for centuries for its unique medicinal properties, it has been rediscovered, recognized and benefited from in the last few years. The active ingredients hidden in its succulent leaves have the power to soothe human life and health in a myriad ways. Aloe Vera is undoubtedly, the nature's gift to humanity and it remains for us to introduce it to ourselves and thank the nature for its never ending bounty.

□□

25

SPECIFIC BENEFITS OF ALOE VERA

Speed healing of first-degree burns, including sunburns. The gel is excellent for easing first-degree burns (including sunburns) and certain minor second-degree burns. If applied after the burn has cooled, it will relieve pain and inflammation and accelerate healing. In one study of 27 people with moderately severe burns, those who used Aloe Vera healed in about 12 days on average, whereas the control group, who covered the affected areas with a regular gauze dressing, took 18 days to heal.

❑ Soothe and hasten healing of cuts, scrapes, and other minor wounds and skin irritations. The gel contains a number of active ingredients, including substances known to help relieve pain, reduce swelling, quell itching, and increase blood flow to an injured area. Some research even indicates that the gel has antifungal, antibacterial, and antiviral properties.

Conversely, Aloe Vera gel may not help treat deeper, infected wounds, or those incurred during surgery. In one study at a Los Angeles hospital, 21 women were given either Aloe Vera gel or a placebo for wounds resulting from a caesarean section or surgery to the abdominal wall. When the gel was used, it took 83 days for the wounds to heal; when the placebo was applied, it took 53 days. (Both groups also received standard anti-infective treatments.)

❑ Lessen painful effects of shingles. Applied gently to the painful lesions that characterize this condition, Aloe Vera gel acts promptly to soothe these sores and provide

26

relief from itching. It also works to decrease the chances that the blisters will become infected.

☐ Reduce symptoms of psoriasis. The ability of Aloe Vera gel to promote healing and quell itching and pain may offer some relief to those who suffer from this troubling condition. In a recent study of 60 people with chronic psoriasis, 83% of those who applied aloe to lesions three times a day for eight months experienced substantial improvement. Only 6% of those using a placebo benefited from its effects.

☐ Ease heartburn, ulcers, diverticular disorders, and other types of digestive upset. A juice made from the Aloe gel acts as an anti-inflammatory and can be taken internally as a remedy for certain digestive complaints. European folk medicine calls for using Aloe Vera juice to relieve heartburn and ulcers.

While there is very little substantive evidence to support these internal uses, preliminary research has shown promising results. In one Japanese study, 17 of 18 patients who took Aloe Vera juice found some relief for their peptic ulcers. However, none of the participants was given a placebo, so comparisons of its effectiveness could not be made. Other clinical trials in Japan indicate that certain compounds in Aloe Vera reduce the secretion of stomach juices and the formation of lesions.

Forms

| ☐ spray | ☐ gel | ☐ lotion |
| ☐ cream | ☐ liquid | ☐ capsule |

Dosage Information *(Special tips)*

☐ As a general rule, keep in mind that products that include 'Aloe Vera extract' or 'reconstituted Aloe Vera' may be much less potent than pure (more than 98%) Aloe Vera. Put another way, be sure to look at the label on any commercial Aloe product to see if Aloe Vera is one of the first few ingredients listed.

❏ For sunburn preparations, confirm that the product contains at least 20% Aloe Vera.

❏ Aloe Vera latex is available in capsule form, usually in combination with other (and more gentle) laxatives.

❏ For burns, cuts, scrapes, shingles, and other skin problems: apply Aloe gel to affected area two or three times a day. For sunburns, you can also add 1 or 2 cups of Aloe Vera juice to a tub of lukewarm water and soak.

❏ For heartburn: drink 2 ounces of juice four times a day.

❏ For ulcers and diverticular disorders: Drink 1/2 cup of Aloe Vera juice twice a day for one month. If you are also taking psyllium for a diverticular disorder, allow at least two hours to elapse before having Aloe Vera juice.

❏ For warts: dab a small amount of fresh or prepared Aloe Vera gel on a compress made of cotton gauze or flannel, and place over the wart. Change the dressing and apply new Aloe Vera daily. Improvement should be evident in three to four days.

❏❏

HEALING BENEFITS OF ALOE VERA

Aloe Vera plant has been known and used as powerful healing plant for eons. There are many healing benefits which are provided by the Aloe Vera plant. The Aloe Vera gel is great 'first aid' for healing wounds and burns. Rubbing the leaves of the Aloe Vera on the cuts in the skin prevents infection and increases the healing process by temporarily act like a bandage. As a result these plants are grown by many people in their homes as houseplants especially in temperate climates.

Used topically the Aloe Vera gel is used as a first aid for sunburns, eczema, burns, insect bites, wounds and treating fungal infections. Aloe is well known for preserving the skin against the harmful effects of the sun's rays. It is helpful in speeding up the healing process of burns and other conditions.

Because of its moisturizing and healing benefits to the skin. Aloe Vera plant is soft sensation when applied giving

shine to the skin and the face. This is why you will find Aloe Vera included in many of the best natural moisturizers, cosmetic and hair products.

Aloe Vera has antifungal properties and is a very good treatment for healing acne, athletes foot, mouth sores and tonsillitis.

Used internally the Aloe Vera gel is useful for poor appetite, stimulating bile flow, bronchial congestion and is helpful in healing a number of digestive disorders such as irritable bowel syndrome. The regular use of Aloe Vera gel and extract keeps the colon clean. Aloe Vera not only provides healing effect to the person but it also returns the bowls to the normal position. Other known benefits occur in the uterus, liver, ulcers, colon and hemorrhoid disorders. As a result it is also used as an herbal remedy for the detoxification and reproductive system.

□□

ALOEA VERA FOR SKIN CARE

Aloe Vera is very helpful in treating various skin disorders.

There are various products available in the market which contain Aloe Vera and makes the skin soft and smooth. They include:

Oats and Aloe Vera Exfoliant

Ingredients

❏ Ground oats-One tablespoon

❏ Ground Almonds-One full tablespoon

❏ Honey-One tablespoon

❏ Aloe Vera gel-One tablespoon

Method

First of all, one should keep all the ingredients in a big bowl and gently mix them. Apply this mixture on the face and neck before performing toning and after cleansing.

The person should apply this mixture by using his hands in circular motions.

When the mixture gets dried, then one should rinse it off with lukewarm water.

This mixture should be applied only after using facial mask.

Silky-smooth Aloe Vera Skin Care Body Cream

Ingredients

- ❑ Lanolin- 1 teaspoon
- ❑ Gel of Aloe Vera- 1 full cup
- ❑ Coconut oil- 1/3 cup
- ❑ Almond oil- ¾ cup
- ❑ Beeswax- ¾ ounce
- ❑ Essential Oil- 1- ½ teaspoon
- ❑ Vitamin E lubricate- 1 teaspoon

Method

First of all, Aloe Vera, lanolin and vitamin E oil should be mixed by using a blender or a food processor. One should take a coconut oil and microwave beeswax in a large container and then heat it for about half a minute and then mix it with other ingredients.

Then the mixture should be again heated for about ten seconds till the large pieces melts completely. Then this mixture should be mixed in almond oil and again heat it if needed. Then use a blender or processor for making it thin. After the mixing of oil, the cream turns into white colour.

Then mix the liquefied oils and if one obtain mayonnaise like constancy, then immediately discontinue the blender or food processor. Then pour the cream into the jars and one can notice that the lotion has become thick. Then apply this mixture on the face which gently absorbs by the skin without leaving any residue on the skin's surface.

Aloe Vera Skin Toner

First of all, a cotton ball should be soaked in an Aloe Vera gel and then apply it on the face to eliminate excess oil and provides freshness to the skin. One can apply this after moisturizer and can use it daily.

It is perfect for normal and oily skin. It one is having sensitive skin, then the gel should be divided into 50 -50 ratio along with spring water. One can also apply Aloe Vera juice.

Aloe Vera Face Mask for Soothing and Healing

Ingredients
- [ ] One drop of Rose essential oil
- [ ] Three tablespoons pure and certified organic Aloe Vera sap
- [ ] One drop of Helycrisum essential oil

Method

All the ingredients should be mixed well and then apply it on the face and neck. Then leave this mixture for few minutes and then wash off with lukewarm water. Let it dry and then apply healing and soothing aromatic blend, which is prepared in a bottle filled with vegetable oil and then mix with one drop of Neroli oil and three drops of lavender oil. It is very helpful for sensitive and dry skin and can be used after taking sunbath.

Exfoliating Foot Mask

Ingredients

- ❒ Half cup of oatmeal
- ❒ Half cup of cornmeal
- ❒ Four tablespoons of Aloe Vera gel
- ❒ Half cup of unscented body lotion

Method

Put all the ingredients in a big bowl then mix them properly. Apply this paste on the feet and rub, beginning from the toes to ankle and then cure it.

for Acne Treatment

Aloe Vera can be used very effectively both internally and externally for so many different things.

But does it work for acne treatment?

Aloe Vera gel is the inner part of the Aloe Vera plant. It has been used for centuries for burns, to heal damaged skin, and for digestive and intestinal problems.

It has proven to accelerate healing because among other things it has the ideal polysaccharides necessary for the skin to repair. It gives the skin the 'building blocks' to repair.

It also accelerates healing of the 'inner skin' the delicate bowel lining.

But should you use it for acne treatment? Does Aloe Vera help acne sufferers?

In one word...YES!

No doubt about it Aloe Vera will help your skin heal from the damage cause by your acne. It will lesson redness and swelling. And it will improve the overall health of your skin.

How to use Aloe Vera for acne treatment?

Get pure Aloe gel and apply liberally topically to your skin after washing. It's as simple as that.

You can use homeopathic medicines after consultation from a renowned homeopathic physician, for quick recovery.

□□

SUNBURN AND ALOE VERA

Sunburn develops injury on the surface of the skin and their effect is long lasting and dangerous. A number of persons notice redness on the skin's surface because of clogged capillaries and swelling which provides blood to the skin.

One should use such sunburn products that include all active curing ingredients and Aloe Vera to protect the skin against injury. People who suffer from sunburn should utilize Aloe Vera gel that contains liquid which are derived from Aloe Vera leaves.

It assists in curing the burns, acts as an antibacterial because it includes Aloectin B that involves encouraging the immune system. Suntan sufferers use Aloe Vera gel in various hospitals. People can purchase pure Aloe Vera gel from the particular stores.

There are large numbers of products that include Aloe Vera such as liquid, lotions, creams and ointments and can be utilized by people who suffer from suntan. It acts like a moisturizer and applied on the burnt area.

One should take a bath or shower and use an Aloe Vera cream or gel on the affected area that will assist people in removing inflammation and pain.

One should use Aloe Vera lotion as it offers about 75% relief from tanning rays and about 90% relaxation from burning rays and does not enable to reach the surface of the skin.

One should take some Aloe Vera leaves and maintain it in the refrigerator and remove the top levels of the Aloe leaves and use on the suntan area. People with mild and medium suntan can take Aloe Vera juice for decreasing the pain and peeling.

Sunburn creates wrinkles on the skin; therefore using Aloe Vera will make the skin beautiful, shiny and glowing. The part of the body because of sunburn should be kept moist with Aloe Vera sap in case of having severe form of sunburn.

There are large ranges of Aloe Vera products which the people can use in case of any skin disorders and protect the surface of the skin from ultraviolet rays.

□□

ALOE VERA FOR HAIR

Aloe Vera is a good way to treat hair loss. Many people use various products that contain Aloe Vera for maintaining thick and healthy hair.

One can apply Aloe Vera gel on the whole scalp is beneficial to treat hair loss.

Actually, Aloe Vera includes the enzyme which is beneficial in stimulating the new hair production. It has properties of anti-inflammatory which are helpful in fighting against Androgenic Alopecia.

Aloe Vera protects the hair and scalp from type of hair problems. A number of people consider that there is no such type of item that can be very useful to prevent hair.

People pay a large amount of money on many hair items and all the items offer no amazing result and have some side effects. Therefore, Aloe Vera is used like the magic material for the production of hairs.

This herb is contained in many hair products such as conditions, hair shampoos and hair oils. An individual can use hair conditioner and shampoo on the whole scalp and then massage it gently and leave it for a few minutes. At last, wash off carefully the hair.

Regular use of Aloe Vera hair conditioner and shampoo prevents the hair loss. Massaging Aloe Vera shampoo on the complete scalp will improve the blood circulation and prevents excess stress and mental labour.

Aloe Vera gel that contains coconut milk with a little quantity of wheat germ oil and then it is utilized like a shampoo and gives amazing results.

Aloe Vera conditioners and shampoo include the best mixture of herbal extracts, natural oils, vitamins and shea butter (a type of fat obtained from the nuts of shea tree). These Aloe Vera items are perfect for all different forms of hair such as oily, dry, thin and normal.

Every conditioner and shampoo is pH balance and is prepared without alcohol or petroleum based ingredients. Aloe Vera jojoba shampoo nourishes and clean hair to make hair healthy and soft and prevents hair loss.

Therefore, Aloe Vera is beneficial for the production of hairs and provides softness and shine to the hair and prevents hair loss and other hair related condition.

Aloe Vera Shampoos & Conditioners

Aloe Vera is an excellent treatment for the hair care. People are utilizing Aloe Vera hair conditioner and shampoo from several years by making the hairs soft and smooth and also make hair healthy and thick.

In reality, Aloe Vera contains the enzyme which is helpful in invigorating the hair's creation.

Aloe Vera contains the ability to fight against Androgenetic Alopecia and also contains anti-inflammatory characteristics which are helpful in the prevention of hair loss.

Aloe Vera hair conditioners and shampoos include the correct blend of vitamins, herbal extracts, shea butter and natural oils. The Aloe Vera product is great for all kinds of hair like dry, thin, normal and oily hair. There are various types of Aloe Vera Hair Shampoo and Conditioners available in the market.

ALOE VERA FOR CONSTIPATION

Aloe is considered as a useful herb which has been utilized for several uses from various years.

It is utilized for both external and internal condition like internal bleeding, burns, skin rashes and ulcers.

It also improves the bowel actions that in turn are helpful to check constipation. There are very susceptible to Aloe Vera.

So, if one suffers from any unnecessary signs or skin rash, then one should immediately stop using it. Aloe Vera contains purgative and laxative action and is helpful in the contraction of muscles.

There are a large variety of products made up of Aloe Vera offered in the market. One must choose a pure Aloe Vera leaves for acquiring excellent results.

So, Aloe Vera juice which is derived from the Aloe Vera latex is best for the people suffering from constipation in order to decrease the disorder.

The patient suffering from constipation can take 2 tablespoon of natural Aloe Vera gel along with juice of apple. The person can also take any other juice also. One can take 1 tablespoon of Aloe drink in the morning or before leaving for bed in the night.

Reduce Constipation with Aloe Vera Capsules

If any person wants to get relief from constipation, then one can acquire Aloe Vera in the type of capsules. These capsules can be taken with another sedative herb like turmeric also. Aloe can also be mixed with fennel seeds powder.

One should only use the pure Aloe Vera in reducing constipation. The Aloe Vera should be obtained only by using hands and not derived from the machines. When Aloe Vera is extracted from the machines, then one can notice yellow juice which is found on the exterior part of the skin of the Aloe Vera leaf that is considered to be impure.

The yellow juice contains laxative and powerful irritating act in the gastronomical region. Studies have proved that Aloe Vera is used to reduce the blood sugar level.

One cannot take other medicines if one is taking Aloe Vera for extended term period. One can also seek the advice of the physician. Aloe Vera has a cleansing action and hence, it reinstates a healthy stability of fine bacteria in the colon.

How to Utilize Aloe Vera to Reduce Constipation?

The person can take Aloe Vera for 5 days and then rest for a while for at least 2 days. One can take Aloe Vera as prescribed by the doctor which can be beneficial for decreasing allergic reactions when applied for long term. It also provides excellent results when used regularly as it has powerful movement in the colon.

Doctors suggested the following doses :

☐ Aloe gel–2 tablespoons per day

☐ Juice of Aloe Vera–One quart per day

☐ Aloe Vera concentrates-5g and takes it at least 3 times in a day.

Caution : Menstruating or pregnant women should avoid Aloe Vera to decrease constipation as it can be dangerous for them.

☐☐

ALOE VERA DRINK

Aloe Vera drink offers relaxation to the persons who are suffered from stomach disorders and impair digestion occurred because of drinking coffee, smoking cigarettes, bad eating habits and because of stress.

Aloe Vera plant includes many substances which are useful and contains minerals, enzymes, vitamins and amino acids.

Aloe Vera drink is obtained with a tasty citrus twist that beneficial to reduce weight rapidly and keep the digestive system healthy.

It is prepared from calming settlement of chamomile with the best quality Aloe.

Features of Aloe Vera Drink

❐ Aloe Vera drink consists of the soothing benefits of chamomile plant.

❐ It is entirely free of a loin.

❐ People can take Aloe Vera drink as a diet supplement.

❐ It is beneficial to lose body weight.

❐ It is made up from premium quality and loaded with vitamins, amino acids and enzymes.

❐ Aloe Vera concentrate needs about 30 servings.

Aloe Vera is supposed to be the most essential vitamins and minerals packaged nutrition drinks. A large number of people take Aloe Vera juice and can utilize it on skin, hair, gums and scalp.

The major uses of this drink are—it offers energy and support skin regeneration, immune function and digestion.

There are many Aloe Vera drink products such as Herbal Aloe Vera Drink and Oleda Aloe Vera Health Drink.

Aloe Vera is prepared from Aloe Vera leaves that include the main parts of the Aloe Vera such as sap, gel and skin. History and Science has shown that if liquid removes from Oleda Aloe Vera Health Drink, people can obtain extra amounts of Aloe elements.

Aloe Vera drink offers significant advantages to the skin of the person and amazing results. It is useful to treat many ailments and diseases. One must take Aloe Vera drink one or two times daily.

Benefits of Aloe Vera Drink

❐ It decreases the swelling of affected skin and also treats skin itching.

❐ It speeds up and increases the general healing while taking it as a tonic.

❐ It is helpful for killing fungus and bacteria.

❐ Aloe Vera drink is beneficial to moisturize skin and make skin smooth and soft.

❐ Aloe Vera drink increases the effectiveness of sunscreen items.

❐❐

ALOE VERA JUICE

Aloe Vera is a member of lily family. There is a yellowish and sticky material in the Aloe Vera leaf.

Aloe Vera plant is beneficial to heal injuries and burns and makes the skin soft and smooth. Aloe Vera comes in the form of gel and liquid in the market. One can obtain it from the specific shops or stores of health and food. The Aloe Vera sap is useful to treat various health problems.

In fact, it can be used as an ingredient in numbers of creams, lotions, gels and shampoos. People can take Aloe Vera juice as a diet supplement or directly.

Method for Making Aloe Vera Juice

Aloe Vera leaves are filleted. And then, green coloured exterior surface of the leaf that contains aloin is separated and remove gel that is scraped from the Aloe Vera leaves.

Aloe Vera gel stays hard while cutting the leaves of Aloe Vera but after a few minutes, an enzymatic effect begins it to turn into the liquid and is short of stinging expire. The requirement for producers of Aloe Vera sap is to regulate the amount of aloin present in the last item for Aloe Vera sap.

Chemical Constitutions

Aloe Vera contains more than 200 biologically active compounds and excess of 70 essentials ingredients. It may contain the following:

- ❏ Enzymes
- ❏ Amino Acids
- ❏ Vitamins
- ❏ Minerals

- ❏ Polysaccharides
- ❏ Proteins
- ❏ Biological Stimulators

Advantages of Juice of Aloe Vera

- ❏ Aloe Vera liquid is consumed for restoring and maintaining balance of stomach acids. It has proved that it promotes and maintains the right equilibrium of stomach acids.

- ❏ Aloe Vera improves digestive functions and absorption of nutrients.

- ❏ Aloe polysaccharides are applied to increase the immune cells property and it is beneficial for eliminating waste and makes toxic and more properties.

- ❏ The sap of Aloe Vera is beneficial to treat digestive system diseases such as irritable bowel syndrome, candida, colitis and acid indigestion.

- ❏ Actually, tissue of Aloe Vera regenerates properties again and make tissue of the large and small intestine, stomach and colon tissue. Many scientists and researchers have shown that this herb simply stimulates the fibroblasts to make fresh tissue. While fibroblasts stimulate, create collagen, proteoglycans and other compounds to make fresh tissue.

Cosmetic Application

- ❏ Body and skin care
- ❏ Regenerates new cells
- ❏ Prevent Wrinkles
- ❏ Treat pimples and acne
- ❏ Remove stretch marks that are occurred due to pregnancy
- ❏ Hair and scalp
- ❏ Prevents dandruff
- ❏ Eye wrinkle remover
- ❏ Protection agent underarm odour
- ❏ Apply it after using shave lotion

ALOE VERA PRODUCTS

Aloe Vera is an essential herb which is used in treating almost every type of disease. People are using herb from several years and prove to be an effective herb. The extract of Aloe Vera gel which is derived from Aloe Vera leaf is used in variety of products. There are different types of Aloe Vera products which are available in the market and they are:

Aloe Vera Colon Cleanse Tablets

It is great blend of Aloe Vera Concentrate, Lactobacillus and herbal extracts. These tablets are very helpful in reducing intestinal disorders and contain cleansing elements to manage digestive promptness.

Caution : The breast feeding and pregnant women should avoid this Aloe Vera product and it is also not suggested for young children.

Aloe Vera Lip Balm

The lip balm prevents the dry, cracked and chapped lips. It is made from the Aloe Vera gel which helps in soothing and moisturizing the lips. It also includes Lysine which keeps the lips healthy. It also prevents the lips of the people form the destructive radiations of the sunrays. One should have a glimpse over the lip balm before using it on the lips.

Aloe Vera Deodorant Stick

This Aloe Vera product is mild, safe and offers long terms safety. This stick is made up of Aloe Vera and does not include alcohol or aluminum chlorohydrate.

Ingredients : Clove, Lavender Oil, Certified Organic Aloe Vera Gel, Corn Starch and Vitamin E.

Aloe Vera Moisturizer Cream

The moisturizer cream contains Aloe Vera and Glycerin. It is great for all kinds of skin which prevents the skin from drying and provides glow to the face.

Aloe Vera Toner

Mostly vegetarians apply this Aloe Vera toner. Aloe Vera Toner contains Aloe Vera, Glycerin and Witch Hazel. It provides softness and freshness to the skin. This is a great product for all kinds of skin.

Aloe Vera Toothpaste

This toothpaste provides oral cleanliness to the teeth. The water contained in along with Aloe Vera sap is connected with a powerful combination of natural ingredients which creates exclusive toothpaste. It also provides freshness to the mouth.

Caution : Vegetarians do not use this Aloe Vera product as it includes marine resource element.

GUIDELINES

The most effective and economical source of the gel is an Aloe Vera plant, which is easy to grow, even on a sunny city window sill. Cut off one of its plumper leaves and wash it off with soap and water. Then slit the leaf lengthwise, and squeeze out the clear gel from the centre. Apply and gently spread the gel on to the painful area and let it dry; repeat the application as needed.

☐ Use common sense when treating a wound; before applying Aloe Vera gel, first clean the area thoroughly.

☐ When buying Aloe Vera juice, check to make sure that the one you select is derived from Aloe Vera gel, not from Aloe latex. Also make sure the juice product contains a minimum of 98% Aloe Vera and that it does not have any aloin or Aloe-emoin compounds, the key substances in Aloe latex.

☐ Be sure to drink Aloe Vera juice between meals.

☐ When shopping for Aloe Vera juice, look for the 'IASC-certified' seal; it is allowed only on products that contain certified raw ingredients that have been processed according to standards set by the International Aloe Science Council, a voluntary certification organization.

☐ Creams and ointments should contain at least 20% Aloe.

General Interaction

☐ Be aware that the long-term use of any laxative, including Aloe Vera latex, can cause you to lose an excessive amount of the mineral potassium. The low blood levels of potassium can be further worsened if you are also taking a potassium-draining diuretic (water-pill) like hydrochlorothiazide or furosemide.

❐ Dangerous heart rhythm abnormalities can develop if you take a digitalis heart medication (like digoxin or lanoxin) along with a potassium-losing diuretic and the Aloe Vera latex. Consult your doctor for guidance.

❐ If you are on oral corticosteroids, such as beclomethasone, methylprednisolone, or prednisone, it is important not to overuse or misuse Aloe Vera juice. A potassium deficiency can develop, and you may experience toxic effects from the medication.

❐ If you are on the oral corticosteroid fludorocortisone (Florinef), it is important not to overuse or misuse Aloe Vera latex. A potassium deficiency can develop, and you may experience toxic effects from the medication.

Possible Side Effects

❐ As a topical treatment, Aloe Vera is quite safe. Occasionally, some people develop a mild allergic reaction marked by itching or a rash. If this occurs, discontinue use.

❐ Due to improper processing, Aloe Vera juice sometimes contains small quantities of the laxative compound in Aloe latex. Should you begin to have cramps, diarrhoea, or loose stools, do not ingest any more of the juice and replace it with a new supply.

Cautions

❐ Don't take an Aloe Vera latex laxative if you are pregnant or breast-feeding; it may trigger uterine contractions. Also avoid using it during a menstrual period.

❐ Children and the elderly should not consume an Aloe Vera latex laxative internally. In addition, laxatives of any kind should never be used by anyone with an intestinal obstruction, an acutely inflammatory intestinal disease (such as Crohn's disease or ulcerative colitis), appendicitis, or abdominal pain of unknown cause.

Ailments & Dosage

Burns : Apply gel to affected areas of skin as needed.

Cuts and Scrapes : Apply cream or gel liberally to wound 2 or 3 times a day.

Heartburn : 2 oz. juice 4 times a day.

Insect Bites and Stings : Apply 4 times a day to bitten area for symptom relief.

Shingles : Apply liberal amount of gel to blistered skin as needed.

Sports Injuries : Apply gel to affected areas 3 or 4 times a day as needed.

Sunburn : Apply gel to affected areas as needed.

Ulcers : Take 1/2 cup juice twice a day for one month.

Warts : Put a pea-sized amount of gel on a compress. Apply as usual.

❏❏

MEDICINAL PROPERTIES OF ALOE

Aloe Vera has very effective in different aliments. The medicinal properties of Aloe are following for various diseases :

Indigestion & Acidity

Take the dried blossom of Tulsi and 5 leaves of Aloe, rind of the Neem tree, black-peppar and peepal in even quantity and grind them to powder form. Take 3 gms. of this powder every morning and evening with plain water. All the acidic effect of the body shall pass out with urine and sweat. But remember, never to take milk over Aloe leaves which might afflict your skin.

Black Spots

These are caused by excessive indulgence in the sexual pleasures which sap your vitality and these black spots appear. Extract a little of juice of Aloe and add two times more lime juice. Make their homogeneous solution and apply this solution or paste over these spots every night with soft hands. The spots will be removed in a week's time. But restrain your sexual urges.

Cataract

Extract the juice of Aloe and add a little of honey to it. Apply this over the eyes every morning and evening. If the cataract is of raw type, it shall be cut away and if it is of ripe type, it shall be ripened soon to enable the doctor to remove it by operation.

Cold and Cough

The chronic patient of this problem have their hair going untimely white. To stop the process and cure it, take 300 gms. of Aloe leaves dried in shade, 50 gms. of Dalchini, 100 gms. Tejpat, 200 gms. saunf (aniseeds), 200 gms. of small cardamom, Banfshaw 25 gms; red sandal 200 gms. and Brahmi herb 200 gms—grind all these ingredients and strain them through a muslin cloth. Now take 10 gms. of this powder and boil it in 500 ml. water and when just a cup of this water remains, add sugar and milk and drink it twice a day like you have tea. All these problems will vanish in a couple of days.

Ear-pain

Take about 10 leaves of Makoy and the leaves of Aloe. Extract their juice together and put it in the affected ear when it is slightly lukewarm (heat it a little in the sun). Alternatively add half a tablet of Camphor in Aloe juice and put this juice in the ear for instant relief.

Eye Troubles

Put a drop of Aloe juice mixed with even quantity of honey for all sort of eye troubles, especially pain and burning. This solution can also be preserved in a bottle. If there is problem of trachoma, grind ten leaves of Aloe together with a clove. Put it into your eyes every four hours. If there is swelling in the eyes, add a little of Aloe-juice with alum and apply it for instant relief.

Epilepsy

Rub Aloe juice over body every day after taking bath. Keep the blossoms of Aloe inside the fold of your hanky every time. At the time of attack, smell the blossom deeply. Should the attack make one unconscious, grind 11 leaves of Aloe and 5 leaves of Basil add a little salt to it and put a few drops of this juice in the patient's nostrils. He would immediately regain his consciousness. Keep a Aloe plant in your verandah or somewhere near your bed room.

Flatulence

Take about 10 ml. of Aloe juice, 10 gms; of dry ginger and 20 gms. of jaggery. Mix all of them together to form small tablets. Take this tablet thrice a day with water to set right your digestive process. But during the period you have this trouble, better keep fast or take only easily digestible food.

Fistula

Have 3-4 Aloe leaves every morning with water. Alternatively take the root of Aloe plant and the fruit of Neem tree (Nimboli) and grind them together. Take 2 gms. of this combination every morning with whey for quick relief.

Flu

Take about 10 gms. of Aloe leaves and 250 ml. of water. Boil them together till water is halved. Now add in the remaining water rock salt, according to taste. No sooner did you start to sweat that the effect of flu shall be removed with the sweat and you shall be alright. Alternatively drink decoction of Aloe leaves, black pepper and batasha for still quicker relief.

Hoarse Voice

Just extract the juice of 10 Aloe leaves, add a little of honey and lick it. Just a small spoonful quantity of this solution will soothen your throat nerves and your voice will be again sweet.

Hair Trouble

Put about 21 leaves of Aloe and 10 gms. of Amla churna in a big bowl. Add a little of water to make a paste of them. Apply it evenly on your head and allow it to dry. Then wash it with cold water. This will prevent hair loss and clear dandruff also.

Heart Troubles

Aloe alongwith Basil is very effective to cure all sort of heart troubles. Since it controls blood presure and keeps blood clean, its regular consumption prevents heart attacks. For especial tonic for heart, prepare the medicine in the following way :

Take 10 Aloe leaves and 10 Basil leaves, about 1 gm. dried powder of Arjun tree and mix even amount of honey. Now either churna or mix them till the solution is fully homogenous. Take 10 Aloe leaves and 10 Basil leaves cord about 1 gm. of this paste, add a little more of honey and lick it at least thrice a day, preferably early in the morning as the first thing, an hour after lunch and as the last thing before retiring for the day.

Hysteria

If the hysteric effect be due to excess of phlegm in the body, make the patient smell Aloe leaves and drink 5 Aloe leaves juice. If it is caused by the excessive heat going to the head, grind five Aloe leaves and five black pepper by mixing them in water and make the patient drink this water every morning and evening for a week's time. The hysteria will be cured.

Indigestion

Take the seeds of Aloe and peepal in equal quantity and grind them to fine powder form. Now add 3 gms. of this powder with a spoonful of honey and lick it twice a day to clear indigestion.

Drinking the tea of Aloe leaves also brings quick relief. The filthy substance will get out of the body with sweat and urine. Alternatively add 1gm. of rock salt in 10 gms. of Aloe leaves' paste and swallow it down with water.

Insomnia

The easiest and best treatment of this problem is to pluck 51 leaves of Aloe. Give to patient just one leave for chewing and spread rest of the leaves evenly below his pillow and the corners of bed below the bed sheet. As the smell of Aloe leaves strikes his nostril, the pereson will feel sleepy and soon he will fall into sleep.

Itching

Extract juice of Aloe and massage on the affected parts of the body. If the trouble is chronic, take about 2 parts of Aloe juice and one part of til oil. Allow them to parboil on low flame. Then cool it and put it in a bottle. This is a most effective oil for all sorts of itching problems.

Jaundice

Add 10 ml. Aloe leaves' juice in about 50 ml. of radish juice. Add a little of jaggery to the combination to sweeten it. Have this solution twice or thrice daily for about a month for getting total relief from this problem.

Alternatively take 3 ml. of Aloe leaves' juice and 3 gms. of the root of Punarnava. Mix them both in 50 ml. of water and drink it for about 15 days. This is a very effective dose to cure Jaundice.

Kidney Troubles

For any type of kidney trouble, Aloe juice provides a very effective cure. Just soak 5 to 7 gms. of Aloe seeds overnight in water. In the morning grind them with sugar and drink the combination. Soon the congestion or infection in kidney will be thrown out by means of copious discharge of urine.

Leprosy

Living in an atmosphere abounding with Aloe and Basil plant is the best treatment. For white patches chew 5 leaves of Aloe every morning, evening and afternoon. Licking the combination of Aloe and Basil leaves' juice with honey will cure the trouble quickly.

Leucoderma

(i) Add a few drops of lime juice in Aloe leaves' juice;

(ii) Grind 10 gms. Aloe leaves and 5 gm of Basil leaves with a clove of garlic and apply the paste on the affected portion every day, 10 days for total relief.

Lethargy

The tea made of Aloe leaves provides instant energy and makes one quite energetic. This is not a cumbersome preposition because as you prepare tea, so you prepare this Aloe tea and instead of putting tea leaves, put Aloe leaves. The regular intake of this tea shall not only provide energy but will also keep you away from all the diseases borne out of the vitiation of phlegm in the body.

Migraine

Get a small bunch of Aloe blossom; dry it in the shade and grind it to powder form. Just take two gms. of it, mix about half a spoonful of honey to it and make the person lick it. God willing, you may never require second dose, for it is a very efficacious treatment. In case you feel like, have another dose by the evening for a total cure.

Mouth boils

Take just a leaf of Chameli plant, and four leaves of Aloe. Chew them properly for a few minutes and suck in the juice. In about a day the trouble will vanish.

Malaria

Take about 10 gms. of Aloe and 5 ml. of Tulsi leaves' juice and add to it 1 gm. of ground black pepper. Administer this dose five or six days after every two hours. Alternatively make small tablets of this combination and feed the patient on Aloe tea additionally. In a couple of days the fever will vanish alongwith the malarial infection.

Night Blindness

Put two drops of Aloe leaves every morning and evening and drink the juice also at three times a day. Continue the treatment for about a month time for relief.

Black pepper is also very effective to cure this trouble. Put some black pepper grains in a wet cloth to allow them to bloat up. Now remove their rinds and grind them in Aloe juice. Line this paste in your eyes every morning and evening for total cure.

Nose-bleeding

The easiest and most effective cure of this trouble is to keep the Aloe blossom near you and smell it as and when you like. For those who are chronic patient of this trouble, this simple treatment is very effective and cures the trouble almost totally. Drinking Aloe juice mixed with honey will also help and provide extra strength to the body.

Paralysis

Boil a few leaves of Aloe in a tumblerful of water.

When cool, strain and put this water in a bottle. Massage this water on the affected limbs. Continue this treatment for at least two weeks. This treatment, coupled with regular intake of the Aloe leaves will produce the desired results.

Pneumonia

Get the pure Tulsi (Basil) oil from a recognised Ayurvedic medicine shop. Put this oil on the chest of the afflicted person. Together with this treatment, extract the juice of five Aloe leaves, mix with it a few ground grains of black pepper at 6 hourly intervel. This combined treatment will produce enough heat in the body to make the person sweat. With sweat all the effect of cold inside the body shall vanish and the patient will be cured.

Chicken Pox

If the person is already afflicted with this problem, then giving Aloe leaves' juice mixed with Ajwain (Bishop's weeds) will provide relief. But to prevent this menace afflicting you or your family members, prepare anti dose tablets in the following way and administer one tablet daily with water.

Take 5 gms. Aloe and 5 gms. of Basil leaves, 2.5 gms. Javitri ½ gm real pearl ash, 20 grains black pepper, ½ gm. saffron and ¼ gm cloves. Add Ganga water to make these tablets.

Spleen Enlargement

Take 5 gms. Aloe leaves dried under shade, 5 leaves of Tulsi and 5 gms. Indra Jau and grind both of them to powder form. Add a little of salt and take the combination with a glass of cold water. Continue this treatment every morning and evening for 10 to 15 days. The effect of Aloe leaves will bring spleen to size and cure the trouble.

Sluggish Liver

Take 5 Aloe leaves, 2 gms. roasted powder of Cumin seeds and 2 gms. of black salt and 5 Basil leaves. Grind them together to make it come in a homogeneous powder form. Add to it even amount of the kernal of the wood-apple. Mix the combination in about 100 gms. of curd to reactivate the sluggish liver. For early relief from any sort of stomach disorder, drink a spoonful of the combination of the juices of the Aloe and ginger.

Swelling in Ears

If there is swelling in the ears, then add juice of Bhangra with the juice of black Tulsi and put a few drops of this juice inside the affected or both the ears for quick relief.

T.B.

Grind together 5 grains of black pepper and five leaves of Aloe leaves. Then mix the combination with half a spoonful of honey and lick it. Make the patient lick this combination twice daily. In winter season, add a little of ginger juice, the husk of wheat and a little of salt also in the combination.This is a very effective treatment but it has to continue quite long. Externally, rubbing a little of Aloe juice and ginger juice's mixture over the lungs shall bring the desired relief. Continue the treatment for about two months. Continue antitubercular treatment too.

Testes Problem

If there is swelling on the testes or any other problem concerning with testes, apply the paste prepared in the following manner over the testes. Take about 5 gms. each of a camel's dung. Amarbel (easily available in Mango groves), the leaves of Arhar and Aloe leaves. Grind them to a homogeneous paste in a little of cow's urine. When the paste is ready, apply it over the testes thickly. Allow it to dry and remove it in the morning. A week's treatment will cure all troubles connected with the testes.

Urinary Problems

For any sort of this trouble, soak about 5 to 7 gms. of Aloe seeds overnight in water. In the morning grind these seeds in water, add a litttle of sugar to the combination to make it more tasty. Drink this combination early in the morning and also in the afternoon, *i.e.*, twice a day. Soon you will have copious discharge of urine and all problems connected with the urinary tract shall vanish in a week's time. Continue drinking raw milk and water mixture at least twice a day also.

Venereal Diseases (Male)

Aloe alongwith Basil leaves juice is very effective to cure all sort of these troubles. Take 5 gms. each of Aloe seeds or dried Aloe leaves and 5 gms. of tamarind. Now add a little of honey to the combination and make small tablets. These astringent tasting tablets should be taken at least four times a day. Don't swallow these tablets but suck it slowly.

If the accompanying cough is of dry type add a little of honey then additionally, make the patient have the combined juice extracted from the even amount of Aloe seeds, ginger and onion. In case of wet-cough add sugarcandy also in the combination.

□□

SOME USEFUL CURATIVE PROPERTIES OF ALOE

Now you are well aware that Aloe has many curative properties. It is very useful in minor troubles.

Headache

Dropping one or two drops of juice of fresh Aloe leaves in the nostrils cures headache..

Baldness

Applying Aloe oil on the bald portion preferably at night and washing the head in the morning stops the failing of other hair and helps in their growth.

Falling & Greying Hair

❒ Washing the hair with water (in which Aloe and Beal or simple Aloe leaves are boiled) stops falling of hair and helps the hair to grow and black and lustrous. This is also useful to kill lices in the hair (Precaution this water should not enter the eyes).

❒ Applying paste of leaves of Beal and Aloe in proportion of 2 :1 on the head and washing after 6-8 hrs. stops hair falling and makes them soft and shiny.

❒ Applying Aloe oil helps in stopping falling greying of hair and makes them black and soft. (Grind Aloe leaves with water and strain it. Mix mustard oil and extracted juice of Aloe in equal quantity and boil it on low flame till all the water evaporates. After cooling store in a bottle for use).

- Applying paste of Neem fruits, leaves of Aloe and washing the head after 3-4 hours helps in eliminating lices and improves growth of hair.

Ear Trouble

Taking the steam of boiled water having Aloe and Neem leaves in it by the ear gives relief in ear-ache.

Dental Troubles

- Using fresh Neem twig piece as brush for cleaning the teeth makes the gums strong, eliminates foul smell and cures pyorrhoea.

- Use of Aloe and Neem tooth powder (Dry the branch of Neem tree with Aloe leaves in shade and burn it. Grind it with little pepperment, salt and cloves and then strain it through a cloth) strengthens the gums and teeth and checks foul smell.

- Drinking and gargling with Aloe water (in which fresh neem leaves are boiled) stops dental decay and pain in the teeth.

- Gargling with Aloe decoction (made with boiling of Aloe and neem leaves, flower, nimboli, root and branches of neem in equal proportion) gives relief to tooth-ache by eliminating infection of gums.

Cough

Gargles with Aloe juice mixed with lukewarm few drops of honey cures cough trouble.

Constipation

Drinking hot water in which 10 gms Aloe leaves have been dissolved early in the morning cures constipation.

Vomiting

☐ Taking Aloe water (Grind 25 gms Aloe leaves mix it in 125 ml. water and strain it) cures nausea and vomiting.

☐ Applying paste of Aloe flower ground with water on the navel portion stops vomiting.

Diarrhoea

☐ Heat inner bark of Aloe tree on Iron *Tava*. Grind it nicely when burnt. Taking a pinch of this powder with curd helps in curing loose motions.

☐ Swallowing powdered Aloe seed and sugar with water controls loose motions.

☐ Taking 10 grounded leaves of Aloe and sugar candy with water checks diarrhoea especially in summers.

Dysentery

☐ Taking Aloe decoction (prepared by boiling Aloe rind in double quantity of water) or 2 gms. ground rind powder with water or honey juice in a day activates the system and controls dysentery.

☐ Taking 10 gms. Aloe juice of leaves in the morning also helps in curing it.

☐ Taking decotion of Aloe leaves (Heat the juice of Aloe leaves on flame cool and strain it) cures dysentery.

Fatigue

☐ Chewing a few Aloe leaves helps in eliminating fatigue.

☐ Eating *Chutney* of Neem and Aloe leaves with little honey in it imparts energy and removes fatigue.

☐ Chewing 5 leaves of Basil and 5 leaves of Neem with Aloe gel and honey gives instant relief and energy.

Itching & Other Skin Ailments

☐ Applying paste of Neem fruits ground with water or Aloe oil on affected part cures itching.

☐ Taking 20 ml of juice of soft fresh Aloe leaves 2 or 3 times a day cures itching caused by impurity of blood.

☐ Taking 30 ml of Aloe juice or 5 gms of Aloe gel with honey cures all impurities of blood.

☐ Applying paste of Aloe leaves mixed with curd on affected part cures ring worm.

☐ Applying Aloe ointment (put a branch with green leaves in boiling mustard oil in an iron utensil. Move it with Aloe stick until it gets thickened into ointment) on the affected part is beneficial for all types of bowls, pustules.

☐ Taking 10 gms of Neem toddy (a type of secretion from certain Neem trees) cures all types of blood impurities and checks skin diseases.

Taking this Neem toddy alongwith Aloe leaves regularly for 6 months to 1 year is helpful in chronic cases of leprosy and other skin diseases.

☐ Taking 5 ml. juice of fresh Aloe leaves and bathing with Neem water (water with Neern leaves boiled in it) helps in curing various skin diseases.

☐ Swallowing 5 gms. powder of dried Neem leaves, Neem flower, Neem fruits and Aloe leaves in equal quantity once in a day cures leucoderma.

☐ Taking fresh juice of Neem leaves regularly stops the pimples and acnes. Applying paste of Aloe gel and Neem oil also cures pimples and acnes.

Digestive and Stomach Ailments

☐ Taking 10 gms of powder (made by grinding rind of Aloe, dry ginger and black pepper—straining it through a fine cloth) with water in the morning for 3 days cures acidity problem.

- Taking 20 ground Aloe leaves, 2 cloves, 3 seeds of Black pepper with little sugar and water twice a day for 2 to 3 days cures indigestion.
- Eating 10-12 ripe Neem fruits and 5 Aloe leaves daily with or after food activates digestive system and normal appetite is resumed. This cures flatulence.
- Taking 3 ml. of Aloe juice in ginger and mint juice 1 ml. each, little Bishop weeds and Black salt and Sendha salt after food cures digestive problems.
- Drinking Aloe water (boil 100 gms of Aloe leaves in 250 ml water and strain it) 2 or 3 times a day helps in regaining normal appetite.
- Taking 4 gms of powder (by grinding green but dry leaves of Aloe) with water 3 or 4 times a day activates appetite and cures dyspepsia.

Stones in Urinary Bladder

Taking 2 gms burnt ashes of Aloe leaves with water breaks the stones, which come out with urine. (Burn the leaves in a utensil after drying them in shade. Cover the utensil, after 4 hrs. grind the leaves).

Piles

- Taking powder made of 3 gms. inside part of the rind of Aloe with 5 gms of jaggery regularly cures piles.
- Applying and rubbing about 5 drops of Aloe oil on the haemorrhoids for 7-8 days helps in curing piles.
- Taking powder of 10 Neem kernels 10 Aloe leaves, little Sendha salt, Gur (jaggery) with fresh water two times a day helps in curing piles.

Leucorrhoea

- Taking the juice of the rind of Aloe with white cumin seeds checks leucorrhoea.

- Drinking cow's milk regularly with little Aloe gel in it at night cures this.

Menstrual Disorders

- Taking juice of 10 fresh Aloe leaves and ginger juice in the same proportion with 10 gms water eliminates and cures excessive pain during menses.
- Taking paste of Aloe leaves (Aloe leaves to be boiled and ground) below the navel will check pain during menses.

Labour Pains and Delivery

- Lying Aloe and neem root in the waist of pregnant woman helps in early child birth. (*Caution*—This Aloe root should be thrown away soon after child is born).
- Taking Aloe water (in which Aloe leaves have been boiled for 15-20 minutes) will make the delivery less painful.
- Taking juice of fresh, Aloe leaves on the Ist day of child-birth helps in contraction of uterus and works as an antiseptic.
- Taking Aloe water (water in which Aloe bark is boiled) when thirsty for the first 6 days after child-birth is good for the mother's health.

Urinary Problems

- Taking 15 gms. juice of tender branches of Aloe with sherbat of unnab or sandalwood twice a day eliminates burning sensation or obstruction in the urinary passage.
- Taking about 20-30 gms of juice of root cures urinary obstruction and burning.

Malaria

- Taking ground 2-3 leaves of Aloe and 2 leaves of Tulsi

and leaves of neem with black pepper on the day of the turn of malaria helps in checking it.

☐ Taking 60 gms ground Aloe leaves, 4-5 black pepper seeds mixed with 120 gms of water twice a day works receded a preventive against malaria.

☐ Massaging the scalp and hair with Aloe oil is also helpful.

Chronic Fever

Taking Aloe water (boil 500 ml. water with 21 Aloe and Neem leaves and 21 black pepper seeds till the water remains 125 ml.) twice a day cures chronic fever.

Arthritis

☐ Massaging the swollen parts and other joints with Aloe oil is very useful. (Boil 50 ml mustard oil and put fresh Aloe leaves in it till it become a bit black. Strain it and keep it in bottle).

Even cooking the food in this Aloe oil is advisable for patients of Arthritis.

Paralysis

Massaging the affected portion with oil extracted from the seeds of Aloe invigorates the dead muscles and tissues.

Diabetes

Taking decoction of rind of Aloe (40 gms of the rind of Aloe to be boiled in 100 ml. water till 30 ml. is left. Strain it) in the morning before breakfast eliminates sugar count in the urine.

Jaundice

☐ Taking 10 gms ground Aloe leaves, 4-5 Black pepper seeds and sugar with water in the morning regularly helps in eliminating the disease.

- Taking ground Aloe leaves and sugar mixed with water after heating it a little cures the disease.

Asthma

Taking 25-30 drops of oil extracted from seeds of Aloe in bettle leaf gives great relief in asthma.

Blisters in the Mouth

Applying Aloe gel on the blisters with cotton cures them.

Sore Throat

Gargling with lukewarm juice of Aloe leaves and water cures soreness of the throat. 5 drops of honey and 2 drops of ginger juice may be added to extract the phlegm and eliminate the infection.

Heart-ailments

- Taking 10 gms juice of Aloe leaves, ground cumin-seeds, mint and Black salt twice a day with lots of water intake during the day eliminates the burning sensation around the heart region.
- Taking Aloe *Chutney* with meals is very useful for controlling bile and stopping burning sensation.
- Taking 1 tsp. of ground seeds of Bakayan tree and ½ tsp of Aloe gel twice a day with water strengthens heart muscles and dissolves cholestrol.

Nose-Bleeding

- . Applying paste of Aloe leaves with little Bishop weeds on the temple stops bleeding.
- Drinking juice of Aloe leaves like Namkeen Sherbat especially in summer is a preventive to those who suffer from nose-bleeding.

Poisonous Insect-bite

Chewing fresh Aloe leaves with or without little salt and pepper helps in eliminating poison.

Worms

❑ Giving 3-4 drops of Neem oil mixed with Aloe gel (Oil) to children and 5 to 6 drops to adults helps in killing the worms in intestines.

❑ Taking 2 tsp fresh Aloe leaves juice with 1 tsp honey kills the worms.

❑ Taking the paste of 1 tsp of juice of fresh Aloe leaves with a little heeng (asofoetida) in it kills the worms.

❑❑

ALOE VERA SIDE EFFECTS

Aloe Vera has many recognized benefits, but what about the Aloe Vera side effects? The Aloe Vera side effects are caused mainly by using the wrong part of the plant. The skin and yellow substance near the skin have long time been used as the active ingredient in laxative products.

Very rarely an allergic reaction may occur. It is usually the 'outer skin' rather than the 'inner filet' that cause the allergic reaction. But like any food it can be a potential allergen.

If you suspect you may be susceptible to an Aloe Vera side effect or allergic reaction then follow these steps.

A Simple Test

Before you use Aloe Vera there is a simple and easy test you can do at home to find out if you are allergic to Aloe Vera gel. Rub a small amount on your inner arm to see if any reaction takes place. If no irritation on the skin is observed then it is generally tolerated. If a burning sensation is experienced wash off with water.

If you do have a reaction the likely reason for this occurring is some of the skin or yellow substance near the skin has been mixed in with the gel during processing. If you purchased an Aloe product then try a different brand.

If you are eating Aloe and have diarrhoea, reduce the amount you eating. Make sure you are drinking plenty of water to help the detoxification process. Then slowly increase the amount you eat over several days until the desired amount is tolerated.

So, while Aloe Vera provides many health benefits to thousands of people long term side effects of using Aloe Vera should not be ignored. If it does occur it is prudent to stop using immediately and consult with your doctor.